S0-BEG-803

DATE DUE

MAR 3		JUN × 2
MAR 3		
MR 2 3 P		
2 L M		

Places in American History

Ellis Island

by Frances E. Ruffin

Reading consultant: Susan Nations, M.Ed., author/literacy coach/consultant in literacy development

WEEKLY WR READER®
EARLY LEARNING LIBRARY

Please visit our web site at: www.earlyliteracy.cc
For a free color catalog describing Weekly Reader® Early Learning Library's
list of high-quality books, call 1-877-445-5824 (USA) or 1-800-387-3178 (Canada).
Weekly Reader® Early Learning Library's fax: (414) 336-0164.

Library of Congress Cataloging-in-Publication Data

Ruffin, Frances E.
     Ellis Island / by Frances E. Ruffin.
          p. cm. — (Places in American history)
     Includes bibliographical references and index.
     ISBN 0-8368-6408-5 (lib. bdg.)
     ISBN 0-8368-6415-8 (softcover)
     1. Ellis Island Immigration Station (N.Y. and N.J.)—Juvenile literature.   2. Ellis Island (N.J.
and N.Y.)—History—Juvenile literature.   3. United States—Emigration and immigration—Juvenile
literature.   I. Title.
     JV6484.R84   2006
     304.8'73—dc22   2005027448

This edition first published in 2006 by
Weekly Reader® Early Learning Library
A Member of the WRC Media Family of Companies
330 West Olive Street, Suite 100
Milwaukee, WI 53212 USA

Managing Editor: Valerie J. Weber
Editor: Barbara Kiely Miller
Art direction: Tammy West
Graphic design: Dave Kowalski
Photo research: Diane Laska-Swanke

Photo credits: Cover, title, pp. 18, 19 © Eugene G. Schulz; p. 4 © Charles E. Steinheimer/Time & Life
Pictures/Getty Images; p. 5 Dave Kowalski/© Weekly Reader Early Learning Library, 2006; p. 6 © North
Wind Picture Archives; pp. 7, 8, 9, 10, 11, 16 © Hulton Archive/Getty Images; p. 12 © Mansell/Time & Life
Pictures/Getty Images; p. 13 © Library of Congress; p. 15 © Topical Press Agency/Getty Images; p. 17
© Henry Groskinsky/Time & Life Pictures/Getty Images; p. 20 © Gibson Stock Photography; p. 21
© Phil Degginger/Getty Images

Printed in the United States of America

1 2 3 4 5 6 7 8 9 10 09 08 07 06

Table of Contents

An Island of Hope 4

Building a Bigger Island 9

Becoming a New American 11

Ellis Island Facts 14

Visiting Ellis Island 18

Glossary 22

For More Information 23

Index 24

Almost half the people living in the United States today have a relative or ancestor who came through Ellis Island.

An Island of Hope

Ellis Island is one of the most famous islands in the United States. More than 12 million people came through this tiny island to live in the United States. It was the first land they stepped on when they arrived in the country. They carried their few belongings and their many hopes for a better life.

Ellis Island lies in New York Harbor. It is near Manhattan in New York City. The Statue of Liberty stands on an island nearby.

Ellis Island is one of many islands in New York Harbor.

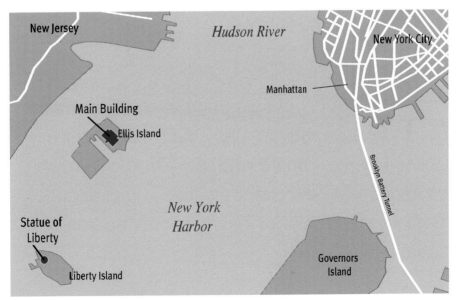

New Jersey

Hudson River

New York City

Manhattan

Main Building

Ellis Island

Brooklyn Battery Tunnel

New York Harbor

Statue of Liberty

Liberty Island

Governors Island

These people in Europe hurried to get on a ship that would bring them to New York.

During the 1800s, people living in other countries began to leave their homes. Many came to the United States. People who move from their own countries to a new one are called immigrants. The largest number of immigrants came from countries in Europe.

Immigrants left their countries for many reasons. Many people were poor. They could not feed their families. Others were treated badly because of their religion.

This man from Ireland (*center*) and woman from Italy (*left*) came to Ellis Island from countries that are hundreds of miles apart. They both thought life would be better in the United States.

Poor immigrants were crowded together on ships.

The trip by ship to the United States took two to four weeks. Many people slept on hard, metal bunk beds. They had few toilets or places to bathe and little food. The air was smelly. Passengers became sick. Some even died during the trip.

Building a Bigger Island

A fort had once stood on Ellis Island. In 1890, the government decided to use the island as a center for immigrants. The government could then know who entered the country.

Before Ellis Island opened, immigrants arrived at a fort named Castle Garden. It was at the tip of Manhattan.

Changes had to be made before the immigrants arrived. The harbor around the island was too shallow for large ships. Workers dug the harbor deeper. Builders also shipped tons of dirt to the island to make it bigger. They put up new wooden buildings.

The first buildings on Ellis Island were made of wood. Later buildings were made from red brick.

Becoming a New American

The government opened Ellis Island as a center to welcome and record immigrants on January 1, 1892. The first immigrant to enter Ellis Island was fifteen-year-old Annie Moore. She had traveled from Ireland with her two younger bothers. Their parents had come three years earlier to find jobs.

Immigrants knew they had arrived in the United States when they saw the Statue of Liberty.

The Ellis Island Immigration Center had many buildings.
Ferries brought immigrants to the Main Building.

Thousands of people arrived in the United States
every day. Most of them came through New York,
the country's biggest port. When their ships
arrived, people took smaller boats called ferries
to Ellis Island.

The immigrants entered the Great Hall in the Main Building. Doctors checked the immigrants to make sure they were not sick. Then government workers asked the immigrants their names and other questions. The immigrants spoke many languages. When the workers wrote down the names, they sometimes made mistakes. Thousands of immigrants entered the United States with a new name.

Government doctors looked at the eyes of the immigrants to make sure they were healthy.

Then most immigrants were given a paper stamped with the word, *Admitted.* They could enter the United States. Other people stayed on the island for weeks or months. Sick people were sent to a hospital on the island. Others had to wait until their families sent them money to travel.

Ellis Island Facts

More than 12 million immigrants entered the United States through Ellis Island. About 3 million of them were children.

Between 1892 and 1924, half the immigrants to the United States came through Ellis Island.

Ellis Island's busiest year was 1907. One million people passed through Ellis Island that year.

The largest number of immigrants came from the countries of Italy, Poland, Russia, Austria, Hungary, Germany, Ireland, and England.

Ellis Island had offices, a hospital, kitchens,
a bakery, a laundry, and a carpenter's shop.
In 1897, a fire destroyed the wooden buildings.
New buildings were made from brick and metal.
The center reopened three years later.

People who had to stay on Ellis Island were given free
meals and a place to sleep.

When Ellis Island closed, its buildings needed repairs.

The government closed Ellis Island in 1954.
In 1965, it became part of the Statue of Liberty
National Monument. People could now visit Ellis
Island, but all they saw were old buildings with
broken windows.

Many people wanted to fix up the buildings on Ellis Island. They wanted visitors to learn about arriving on Ellis Island. During the 1980s, they raised $160 million. The Main Building on the island became The Ellis Island Immigration Museum. It opened on September 10, 1990.

The museum in the Main Building celebrates four hundred years of immigration to this country.

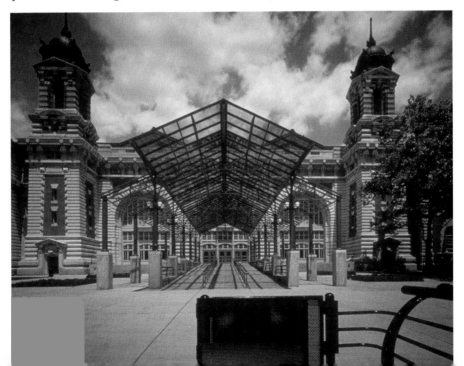

Visitors enter the same doors that greeted the immigrants.

Visiting Ellis Island

Two million people visit Ellis Island every year.
Like the immigrants, they take a ferry to the island.
Only the large Main Building of the museum is
open to visitors. They can see photographs,
clothing, toys, papers, and other items that
belonged to the immigrants.

The first exhibit people can see is the baggage room on the first floor. Trunks, suitcases, and baskets that belonged to immigrants fill a large glass box. Visitors also can look at maps that show the countries the immigrants left. Other maps show where large groups of immigrants settled in the United States.

Immigrants sailed across the ocean to a new life with only the few belongings they could fit in a suitcase or basket.

On the second floor stands a statue of Annie Moore, the first immigrant on Ellis Island. In the Oral History Listening Room, on the third floor, people can listen to tapes of immigrants telling their stories. Many of these immigrants were children when they came here.

Visitors can learn about the people who make up the United States.

Before leaving Ellis Island, visitors stop at the Wall of Honor outside. The names of 600,000 immigrants are cut into the wall. It honors people who dared to leave their homes and move to a strange land. Ellis Island reminds us of their journeys and their hopes.

If your relatives came to the United States, their names can be added to the Wall of Honor, too.

Glossary

ancestor — a family member from the past farther back than grandparents

baggage — suitcases and containers used for carrying clothes and other items when traveling

carpenter — a person who makes buildings and objects from wood

exhibit — something put on display

ferries — boats used to take people, cars, and goods across water

immigrants — people who come to live in a new country after leaving their homes in another country

immigration — the movement of people from one place to another

monument — a building or place made to honor and remember people or events

oral — spoken instead of written

port — a place located on a body of water where ships can load and unload

For More Information

Books

Dreaming of America: An Ellis Island Story. Eve Bunting
(Troll Communications)

Ellis Island. First Facts (series). Terri Degezelle
(Capstone Press)

Ellis Island. A True Book (series). Patricia Ryon Quiri
(Children's Press)

Ellis Island. Wonder Books Level 3 Landmarks (series).
Cynthia Klingel (Child's World)

Web Sites

American Family History Immigration Center
www.ellisisland.org
Search for records of your ancestors; add a name to the
Wall of Honor.

Ellis Island Immigrants
www.ellisislandimmigrants.org/ellis_island_immigrants.htm
Facts and figures about Ellis Island and immigration

Index

buildings 10, 12, 15, 16, 17
Castle Garden 9
Ellis Island Immigration
   Museum 17, 18, 20
Europe 6, 7, 14
exhibits 19, 20, 21
ferries 12, 18
government 9, 11, 13, 16
Great Hall 13
hospital 14, 15
immigration reasons 7

journeys 8, 21
languages 13
Main Building 13, 17, 18
Moore, Annie 11, 20
New York City 5, 12
New York Harbor 5, 10
passengers 8
ships 6, 8, 10
Statue of Liberty 4, 5,
   11, 16
Wall of Honor 21

About the Author

Frances E. Ruffin has written more than twenty-four books for children. She enjoys reading and writing about the lives of famous and ordinary people. She lives in New York City with her son, Timothy, a young writer who is writing his first novel.